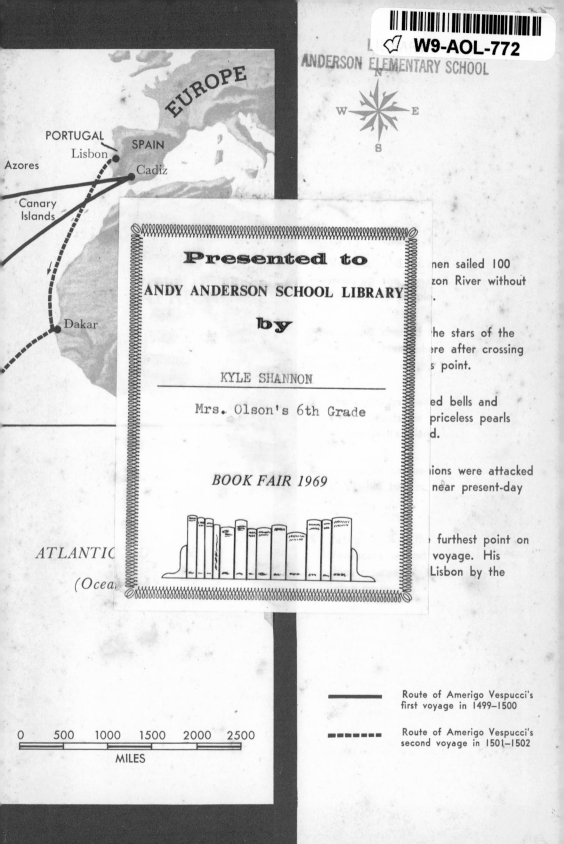

EUROPE

PORTUGAL
Lisbon   SPAIN
Azores   Cadiz

Canary
Islands

Dakar

ATLANTIC

(Ocea

...men sailed 100
...zon River without
...

...he stars of the
...ere after crossing
...s point.

...ed bells and
...priceless pearls
...d.

...ions were attacked
...near present-day

...e furthest point on
...voyage. His
...Lisbon by the

0   500   1000   1500   2000   2500
MILES

——————— Route of Amerigo Vespucci's
first voyage in 1499–1500

- - - - - - - Route of Amerigo Vespucci's
second voyage in 1501–1502

THE ASTROLABE, an instrument developed by the Greeks, is the symbol for World Explorer Books. At the time of Columbus, sailors used the astrolabe to chart a ship's course. The arm across the circle could be moved to line up with the sun or a star. Using the number indicated by the pointer, a sailor could tell his approximate location on the sea. Although the astrolabe was not completely accurate, it helped many early explorers in their efforts to conquer the unknown.

World Explorer Books are written especially for children who love adventure and exploration into the unknown. Designed for young readers, each book has been tested by the Dale-Chall readability formula. Leo Fay, Ph.D., Professor of Education at Indiana University, is educational consultant for the series. Dr. Fay, an experienced teacher and lecturer, is well known for his professional bulletins and text material in both elementary reading and social studies.

A WORLD EXPLORER

Amerigo Vespucci

BY FAITH YINGLING KNOOP

ILLUSTRATED BY TED LEWIN

GARRARD PUBLISHING COMPANY
CHAMPAIGN, ILLINOIS

To young explorers
of their own New World—
Kevin, Mikel and Kathy

This series is edited by Elizabeth Minot Graves

Contents

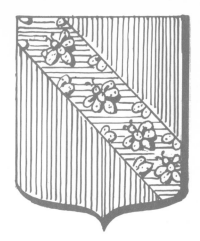

1

Daydreams

"Amerigo! Amerigo Vespucci!"

The ten-year-old boy lay on the hilltop, staring into the blue Italian sky. The voices seemed to come from his dreams.

A puffy cloud looked like a church dome. "That is our church in Florence," Amerigo whispered. "Now it's changing into a white ship on a blue sea. Why do clouds change? Where do they come from?"

"Amerigo!" Suddenly he knew it was his father calling. It must be time to go home, after a day in the country. It was springtime, 1464.

"Here I am!" Amerigo shouted. He sat up, rubbing the daydreams from his eyes.

Father Vespucci's dark head appeared above the hilltop. His anxious frown turned into a smile. He called to those below, "Amerigo is found!" Then he frowned again. "Why did you run away?"

"I didn't mean to run away." Amerigo shook his head. "I just wanted to climb the hill. I didn't think anyone would miss me."

"Your uncles, your brothers, and all the people in the village are looking for you," his father scolded. "Why didn't you answer our calls?" He sat down, panting, beside the boy in the grass.

"Because—" Amerigo stopped. Would his father understand? He went on truthfully, "Because the voices seemed to come from the clouds. Father, what are clouds? And what are stars? Is the earth really round?"

"Come," his father laughed. "Only a scientist could answer all of the questions you ask."

Father and son started down the hill. "I love my four sons and one daughter alike," the father said. "But when you were lost, Amerigo, I felt as if I had lost everything. For God gave you the best mind in the family. If you use it well, you will become famous."

Amerigo was surprised. He started to ask a question. But they were in the village now and Amerigo's brothers were running to meet them.

"Where were you?" asked the oldest, Antonio.

"Why did you run away?" asked Girolamo, who was eleven.

"Why didn't you take me?" cried nine-year-old Bernardo.

"I only climbed the hill," laughed Amerigo. "You three boys are too lazy to climb hills!"

The boys trooped over to the village inn. It belonged to an uncle. "Good-by!" they shouted. "We're going home!"

The four brothers piled into a square donkey cart. Their father rode another donkey. They were soon at their home in Florence. It was a big stone house on the River Arno.

Amerigo looked up at the coat of arms over the door. The same marker was on Grandfather Amerigo Vespucci's house

next door. Each important family in Italy had its own coat of arms. The Vespucci design was a red shield with a blue band. Gold wasps, or "vespa," for "Vespucci" flew across the shield.

"Wasps are busy workers," Father once told the boys. "They sting if anyone bothers them."

The boys' mother greeted them as they entered the house. "You are late," she said. She shook her head. "You always stay too long in the country."

Their little sister came running. "I wanted to go too," she wailed.

Amerigo gave her a quick hug. But he was still thinking of his father's words on the hillside: "You will become famous."

"Famous? How?" Amerigo wondered. His father and grandfather were well-known in Florence, in both business and government. But Amerigo did not want to be a businessman or enter government work. He wanted to study the stars and the great world he lived in.

"Only a scientist could answer your questions," his father had said.

"So," Amerigo decided, "I shall be a scientist."

2

Carnival Nights
and Schooldays

"It's fun to be last in a parade," Amerigo laughed. "This way, we see it all as it starts." Amerigo, now in his teens, stood on the street with a crowd of boys.

"Look!" cried one of Amerigo's brothers.

He pointed to a beautiful float pulled by white horses. It was covered with tinkling silver bells and cupids. The coats of arms of the Benci and Strozzi families were in the center of the float. Bartolommeo Benci was having a parade to honor his sweetheart, Marietta Strozzi.

Gaily dressed musicians with flutes and trumpets marched. Next rode Bartolommeo himself and eight friends. They were on prancing horses with silk coverings.

"Cousin Piero!" shouted Amerigo. A horseman dipped his gold and silver lance in answer. His velvet robe and cape were covered with pearls.

Amerigo and his friends fell into line behind the horsemen. The parade wound through crooked streets to Marietta's house.

Marietta stood on a balcony lit by four flaming torches. Bartolommeo galloped to the balcony, waving his feathered cap. Marietta threw Bartolommeo a lacy scarf.

At last the parade turned away. Then it went off to honor other horsemen's sweethearts. It ended with a party at the Benci mansion. The sun was rising when the Vespucci brothers returned home.

Amerigo quickly changed into his school clothes. He set out for Saint Mark's monastery school. Uncle Giorgio Vespucci, a monk, was his teacher there.

Amerigo hoped today's lessons would be on the stars and geography, his favorite studies. Perhaps Uncle Giorgio would tell about the teachings of his friend, Dr. Paolo Toscanelli. Dr. Toscanelli was the best mapmaker in the world. He wrote about the sciences Amerigo loved.

As he walked, Amerigo's thoughts kept slipping back to the parade. What fun parades and carnivals were! Holidays, weddings, birthdays, victories in war—all called for gay celebrations in Florence. Florence was the richest city in Italy. It had the best art, music and books in Europe. Florence was a wonderful place!

Amerigo's steps slowed. He was very sleepy. But he would not miss school for anything.

In Saint Mark's, Amerigo sat down at a table. "Open your Latin notebook," Uncle Giorgio said.

Amerigo was disappointed. His Latin was not as good as his science.

"Write this in Italian and in Latin," Uncle Giorgio's gentle voice went on: "Hate evil governments. Be honest always."

Amerigo yawned. The pen fell from his hand. His head dropped. He was fast asleep.

"Amerigo!" The voice was no longer gentle. Amerigo jerked awake. Uncle Giorgio's round, black eyes blazed.

"I—I was a torch bearer last night in the Benci parade," the boy began.

"And there was a dinner?" asked Uncle Giorgio.

"Oh, yes. There were pigeons, blackbirds, chickens, turkey, wines, fruit and sweets. Everything was served on gold and silver plates."

"You feasted while beggars starve in the city streets!" Uncle Giorgio's voice shook with anger. "And you sleep, when you have so much to learn!"

"My brothers stayed home from school today to sleep," Amerigo put in.

"Your brothers, pah!" Uncle Giorgio growled. "They are dull, good boys. You, with your brains, can do great things for the world. But if you waste your time at parties, I can teach you no longer."

"I'm sorry, Uncle Giorgio. Please keep on teaching me," Amerigo begged.

"Go home now," Uncle Giorgio ordered. "Get some rest. Come back when you are ready to study."

Amerigo went home full of good intentions. He would give up parades and parties and study hard. But it was not always easy to keep his promise. He loved fun as well as science.

A few years later Amerigo was older and more serious. He wrote in his notebook, "Arise early in the morning and sleep not so much, young man who . . . has too much played the fool, dancing and frolicking! Do not loll around . . . in idleness, but tire thyself out a little."

Amerigo wrote on, "My father anxiously desires that I seek out and learn those things which may help me to win fame and honor . . . I have now decided not to lose more time. I shall conquer myself and I shall . . . put aside from me . . . pleasures and give true signs of virtue."

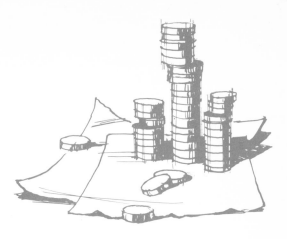

3

Amerigo Goes to Work

A group of horsemen came to a stop on the sunny hilltop. "Florence!" Amerigo pointed to the beautiful city below. "It's good to be home."

"You did not like your two years in Paris?" his Uncle Guido Vespucci asked.

Amerigo, now 27, flashed his boyish smile. "It was exciting, living there with you, Uncle Guido. Who wouldn't like being secretary to the Ambassador from

Florence? I enjoyed meeting King Louis and the leaders of France. I learned horsemanship and French."

"And you learned how to act in a king's court and how to write polite business letters," Uncle Guido added.

"But there was no chance to learn more about science." Amerigo shook his head. "I'm behind with my scientific studies."

"So you won't go to Rome with me for my next job." Again Amerigo shook his head. The older man sighed. The horsemen galloped on into Florence.

Amerigo could hardly wait to reach the Vespucci home. There he found his father sick in bed. "Amerigo!" his father cried, holding out his arms. "Welcome home! Tell me everything about your work in France for Lorenzo the Magnificent, ruler of Florence." He hugged his son.

"As I wrote you, Father, it was wonderful," Amerigo smiled. "But now I'm staying home, to—"

The father broke in, "Good! I need you to carry on my business. I can no longer look after my family affairs and my government work too."

Amerigo drew a deep breath. He had wanted to spend all his time studying science. "I'll be glad to carry on the Vespucci business," he answered slowly.

Now Amerigo hurried to Saint Mark's to see Uncle Giorgio. Uncle Giorgio, too, threw his arms around Amerigo. "Did you keep up with your science in France?" he asked.

Amerigo's answer was no. "Are there any new discoveries about the stars or any new maps?" Amerigo began eagerly. "How is Dr. Toscanelli?"

"One question at a time," Uncle Giorgio smiled. "Dr. Toscanelli is very weak, but he still teaches in his home. He still writes and draws maps. Come, I know you would like to see his famous map again."

Uncle Giorgio pulled a large map roll from a shelf. He unrolled it on a table and weighted the corners with pieces of marble.

Amerigo leaned over the map. He traced a line west from Europe across the Ocean Sea, which today is the Atlantic Ocean. He pointed to the Indies, as India, China and Japan were then called. "Is anyone planning to cross the Ocean Sea looking for the Indies?" he asked. "I know Dr. Toscanelli thinks it is possible."

Uncle Giorgio nodded. "Remember Christopher Columbus, that Italian seaman who wrote to Dr. Toscanelli?

Columbus has a copy of this map. He wants to sail west to the Indies. He is in Portugal now. He hopes the King of Portugal will give him ships.

"Thirteen hundred years ago," Uncle Giorgio went on, "the Egyptian scientist Ptolemy said that the world was round. That will be proved if Columbus can sail west to the Indies."

Soon Amerigo was hard at work in his father's business. Keeping accounts, collecting money and paying bills were not very exciting. He longed to have more time to study. Before the year was over his father died.

In Italy, when a father died, his oldest son usually became head of the family. But Father Vespucci's will made Amerigo the head, instead.

So Amerigo had to settle his father's

affairs and look after the family. He was so busy that visits with Uncle Giorgio were short. They were sad, too, for Dr. Toscanelli had just died.

One day Amerigo had a visitor. "Lorenzo!" Amerigo exclaimed. "Welcome!"

Lorenzo di Pier Francesco de Medici was a younger cousin of the ruler of Florence. He was a merchant and banker, a rival of the older Lorenzo. "I need an honest manager for my business and farm," began Lorenzo. "He would live in my palace in Florence. He would travel to other cities." Lorenzo finished, "Amerigo, you are just the man I want."

Amerigo gasped. Lorenzo's palace had a famous library full of the world's greatest books. Amerigo could read them. He could travel through all of Europe. "Thank you," he said. "I will accept."

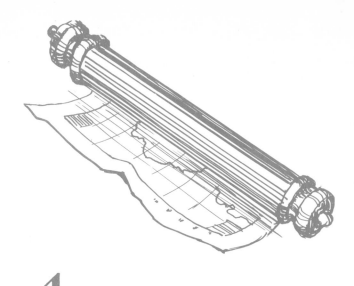

4

The Map

Amerigo liked his new work. He mapped trade routes for Lorenzo's ships in the Mediterranean Sea and along the Atlantic coast. He ordered goods from Asia and had them sent to ports in Europe. There he bought other goods in return.

The people in Europe needed many things from the Indies. Pepper, cloves and other spices were needed to flavor the tasteless dried meat. Perfumes were needed too. They covered the smell of garbage dumped in the city streets. It was thought that perfumes would ward off disease. Drugs and medicines were also needed. Spices, perfumes, drugs and jewels came from the Indies.

The Turks refused to let Europeans travel through their land to the Indies. Lorenzo's ships had to go to Turkey or Egypt and buy Oriental goods there. The Turks added high taxes to the price of the goods.

One day Lorenzo came into Amerigo's office. Amerigo looked up from his desk and sighed. "If only we could sail west to the Indies as Columbus hopes!" he said.

"The taxes placed by the Turks have become so high! Only the rich can buy Eastern goods now."

Lorenzo nodded. Then he said, "I hear that the Portuguese king refused to send Christopher Columbus across the Ocean Sea. Columbus is now in Seville, Spain. He hopes to get ships from the King and Queen of Spain."

"I do hope he gets them," Amerigo said. "A short route to the Indies would help our business. We need to make up the money we've lost in Spain. Look!" He held out an account book to Lorenzo.

Lorenzo frowned at the figures. Then he said, "These figures can't be right, Amerigo. Our agent there must be cheating us." Lorenzo decided to send Amerigo to Seville. Amerigo was to get another agent if he thought best.

Amerigo sailed for Spain. He found that the agent in Seville was a cheat. Amerigo hired another man in his place.

The new agent was Gianetto Berardi, an Italian living in Seville. He was an older man, with a gray, pointed beard. For years, Berardi had provided ships with food and trading goods for Mediterranean voyages. His payment was a share of the goods brought back from faraway ports. Berardi was a good trader and as honest as Amerigo himself.

Many Italians lived in the beautiful city of Seville. It was not long before Amerigo met Christopher Columbus. "I am Amerigo Vespucci of Florence," he told the tall, red-haired man. "I knew Dr. Toscanelli, whose map you have."

Amerigo and Columbus became friends at once. They talked about Dr. Toscanelli

and about the famous Italian traveler, Marco Polo. Two hundred years before, Marco Polo had traveled overland to the Indies and had written of their riches.

"I am sure the Indies lie west across the Ocean Sea," Columbus said. "But the Spanish King and Queen cannot decide whether or not to give me ships. They fear the ocean is too wide to cross."

Soon Amerigo had to return to Florence. He missed his talks with Columbus, but he enjoyed the famous men he met in Lorenzo's palace. He learned something from everyone, and much from the books in the library. He still studied astronomy and geography with Uncle Giorgio.

One night there was a dinner at the palace. A scientist asked Lorenzo and his friends, "Have you seen Velasco's famous map of the world? Its owner is willing to sell it, but he wants 130 gold ducats."

"I'm sure it's worth it," Amerigo cried. "I have heard that it is the most accurate map that has ever been drawn."

The next day Amerigo hurried to see the map. The owner unrolled the large piece of parchment. It showed the known world from the Atlantic or Ocean Sea to Arabia. It showed Europe, North Africa, part of the Red Sea and the Persian Gulf. Seas were painted green, lowlands golden and mountains blue. On the border were red decorations and pictures of kings and flags. Amerigo drew a deep breath. "It is the best map I have ever seen," he murmured. "Even though it is so costly, I must have it."

Amerigo bought the map. He took it to show Uncle Giorgio. They studied the great drawings together. "It will help me plan trade routes," Amerigo told his uncle.

Uncle Giorgio smiled. "Your father and I always spent too much on books. But books and maps are more worthwhile than jewels."

Amerigo picked up the map. He bent it into a great tube with the drawing outside. "This shows how Columbus plans to sail west across the Ocean Sea to the Indies."

Uncle Giorgio nodded. "Perhaps you, too, may sometime map the world," he answered. "For you are becoming a real scientist."

5

Seville, City of Explorers

Several years passed. Amerigo was again in Seville on business. He was helping his friend Gianetto Berardi. There was too much work in Seville now for one Medici agent to handle.

Spain had won a long war against the Moors. There was money now for exploring new lands and seas. The King and Queen were sending Columbus across the Ocean Sea with three ships. Berardi was one of those who was outfitting the ships.

Besides working for the Medicis, Berardi
was also in business for himself. He
bought trading goods with his own money,
to sell at a profit. "I am paying one fifth
of Columbus' expenses," Berardi told
Amerigo. "It is a big gamble for me."

Columbus' ships were at the seaport of
Palos. Sometimes Columbus came to
Seville to see about his supplies. Amerigo
went over the supply lists with Columbus
and Berardi. "Salted meat, cheese, onions,

sardines, oil and vinegar, rice, garlic, salt, honey and cereal have all been ordered," Amerigo said, reading a list aloud.

"And there must be tools to repair the ships and trinkets to trade with the Asians," Berardi added.

"You think of everything," Columbus smiled. "I'll bring back treasure to pay for this, many times over."

Columbus sailed from Palos in August, 1492. Amerigo and Berardi were thrilled, but anxious. Berardi told Amerigo, "Many people say that Columbus and his men are crazy and will never return. If that happens, I will lose everything."

Amerigo was now living with Berardi. He was busy increasing the Medici business.

That fall and winter, Amerigo and Berardi waited for word of Columbus. There was none. In February, Amerigo told the worried Berardi, "When spring comes Columbus will return."

Then, one day in March, 1493, Amerigo burst into the house shouting, "Columbus has returned to Palos! He found islands off the coast of the Indies! He will stop on his way to see the King and Queen!"

In a few days a great parade stopped at Berardi's very door. There were sun-tanned seamen and ten brown-skinned savages. Columbus called them Indians

because he had found them in what he believed to be the Isles of the Indies. There were parrots and treasures. And there was Columbus himself.

"Only six of the Indians are well enough to travel to Barcelona," Columbus said. "May I leave the others with you?"

Amerigo was delighted. By signs he showed the Indians he was their friend. But they puzzled him. These people were brown skinned, with large, brown eyes. Marco Polo had said the Orientals were yellow, with black, almond-shaped eyes. Why were these island Indians so different from other Orientals?

Soon Amerigo and Berardi were busy outfitting a second voyage for Columbus. "If I were a seaman," Amerigo said, "I'd go with Columbus. I must learn to sail a ship so I can explore, too."

But Amerigo did not have much time to learn seamanship now. Before Columbus returned from his second voyage, Berardi died. He left Amerigo, his "agent and especial friend," to settle his affairs.

Now Amerigo made an important decision. He would make his permanent home in Seville. Seville was interested in backing explorers. Men of science came here, as they had once come to Florence. Now the people of Florence were torn by wars, and the two Medici families were enemies. Even Amerigo's own family was divided. Peace-loving Amerigo was glad to stay away from the quarrels.

Also, Amerigo had fallen in love with a lovely Spanish lady, Maria Cerezo. He had married her and they lived in a house built around a flowery courtyard. Soon Amerigo's nephew, Giovanni, came from Florence to live with them. He was brother Antonio's son, and wanted to study science with Amerigo. Twelve-year-old Giovanni was bright-eyed and quick to learn. Before long, he was like a son to Amerigo.

As more explorers crossed the Ocean Sea, Amerigo studied navigation. He learned the use of the seamen's guiding instruments — the quadrant and the astrolabe. From his astronomy he already knew how to steer a ship by the stars. He also knew how to map new lands. And from his work, he knew what was needed on a long voyage.

One evening Amerigo told Maria and Giovanni, "I have asked the King and Queen to let me sail across the Ocean Sea. I want to make the first scientific study of the islands of the Indies."

6

New Lands and Stars

Amerigo was thrilled. His orders had come from King Ferdinand and Queen Isabella. He was to sail to the Indies. A fleet of four ships was ready, commanded by Alonso de Ojeda. Alonso had been with Columbus on his second voyage.

Columbus had now made three voyages to the Indies. But he had found only the simple island homes of brown savages.

Where were the rich cities of Japan and China? Where were the gold roofed palaces that Marco Polo had described? Where were the educated yellow people in jeweled silk robes? "Find the places and people," the King told Amerigo. "Make maps of your discoveries. And bring back treasure."

On May 18, 1499, Amerigo sailed from Cadiz. In a week, the ships landed at the

Canary Islands off the coast of Africa. There they got water, food and wood.

Amerigo and Captain de Ojeda stood on the dock. "I sail first to Margarita Island for pearls," the young captain said. "It is off the Pearl Coast discovered by Columbus." Today this is the coast of Venezuela in South America.

"I shall sail farther south," Amerigo said, smiling down at the short, handsome

captain. "I hope to find the Indies' south coast. I shall chart new lands, stars and waters. I'll get pearls on my way back."

The two leaders parted on the Ocean Sea, each with two ships. Amerigo would explore. Alonso would seek treasure.

After 24 days of smooth sailing, Amerigo heard a lookout cry, "Land!" The men cheered and sang thanks to God.

"Lower the boats!" Amerigo ordered. He had been charting their course with the astrolabe. He knew this land was farther south than the land Columbus had explored. It was today's Brazil.

Six in a boat, Amerigo's men rowed toward a thick, green jungle. Bright songbirds darted through tree branches. Monkeys chattered. The perfume of flowers, fruits and damp earth filled the air. But there was no place to land.

Some rowboats became stuck in the mud.
Amerigo ordered them back to the ship.

"Follow the coast south!" Amerigo told
the pilots.

The sea was no longer blue, but
muddy. The men drew up pails of brown
water. Amerigo sipped a little. "It is
fresh," he cried. "We must be at the
mouth of a great river."

The ships followed the coast into a great gulf 150 miles wide. They sailed inside the gulf for 100 miles. Here, where the river was sixteen miles wide, the ships dropped anchor. Amerigo thought this must be a river of Asia. Today it is called the Amazon, in Brazil.

Amerigo and twenty armed men set out in rowboats, with enough food to last four days. They rowed upstream for two days, 72 miles. They found no opening in the swampy jungle, no people, no houses. But sometimes they saw smoke rising behind the green curtain of trees.

After the rowboats returned, the ships sailed on south. One night Amerigo saw the North Star barely peeping above the horizon. Farther south, the next night, the North Star did not show at all. Amerigo had crossed the equator. It was the most exciting thing that had ever happened to him. But his men slept on. None of them cared about being the first Europeans to cross the equator here.

The ships sailed for 100 miles up another river. It was a river later called the Pará. Still there were no people. But butterflies, huge beaked birds (toucans) and parrots dotted the trees with bright color. The explorers called this country, "Land of Parrots."

Amerigo became more excited with every mile. Such great rivers could only come from a great continent. The continent must be Asia. But where were Marco Polo's golden cities?

On and on the two ships sailed southeast, for 800 miles. Now they found themselves in a strong ocean current, running from southeast to northwest. Amerigo studied the current and put it on his map. The current slowed the ships so much that the men began to complain. "Where are the pearls we were to find?" they demanded.

Amerigo was excited about exploring new lands. He had almost forgotten treasure hunting. Sadly he gave the order, "Turn back! Head northwest for the Pearl Coast!"

7

The Pearl Coast

Amerigo's ships soon recrossed the equator. They sailed along the northern coast of South America. They went past Brazil and the Guianas. They passed the mouth of another great river, the Orinoco. "Here is another proof that this is surely the continent of Asia, and not a small island," Amerigo said.

One morning three mountain peaks on the island of Trinidad loomed ahead.

They had been named by Columbus. "We shall land here," Amerigo said, "and look for pearls."

A crowd of Indians welcomed the explorers. The natives led the visitors to their village for a breakfast of delicious fruits, fish and bread. But they had few pearls to trade. So Amerigo sailed west along the Pearl Coast, as Venezuela was then called.

Soon the ships reached the island of Margarita. This was the place De Ojeda had headed for two months ago. Amerigo and his men landed and showed the Indians tiny bells, mirrors, bright beads and brass ornaments. By signs, they asked to trade these for pearls. "Each of the natives was willing to give all the pearls he had, for one of our bells," Amerigo wrote later.

The Indians jingled and smelled the trinkets. They especially liked the smell of brass. They tied bells onto their hands, arms, legs and ankles. They laughed and danced about. By signs, they promised to dive for more pearl oysters. But Amerigo was eager to explore further west.

Friendly natives greeted the explorers at one landing after another along the Venezuelan coast. In the forests the Spaniards saw wildcats, deer, wild pigs and rabbits. But where were the Indies' tigers and elephants? Once Amerigo and his men came upon a huge snake. "It is as big around as a man's waist!" Amerigo cried. They ran to their boats.

Later, near today's city of Caracas in Venezuela, Amerigo's men met hostile natives for the first time. They were attacked by many natives shooting arrows.

In spite of their heavy armor, many Spaniards were wounded. A great battle was fought on the shore. The Spaniards drove the Indians back and burned their houses. But the ships had to stay in the harbor twenty days, while the ships' doctor cared for the wounded. One Spaniard died.

While the ships were at anchor, Amerigo could sleep by day. Each night he mapped the stars. From them, as pilots before him had done, he found the exact latitude of his ships. Latitude is one's distance north or south of the equator.

Now Amerigo wanted to find longitude by the stars. Longitude is the distance east or west of an imaginary north-south line on the earth. If a seaman could tell both latitude and longitude, he would know exactly where his ship was at all times. Here, in the quiet harbor, Amerigo did learn to tell longitude by the stars. Scientists said later that this was one of the world's greatest discoveries.

At last Amerigo's men were well enough to sail west. They stopped along the Venezuelan coast and on nearby islands. They called today's island of Curaçao the "Isle of Giants" because of the tall Indians there. They called today's island of Aruba, "Little Venice" or "Venezuela." This was because its houses were built on poles in the water, like those in Venice, Italy. Later the country of Venezuela was given this same name.

Amerigo's ships were leaking badly, so the explorers headed north to repair them. They reached the great island of Hispaniola discovered by Columbus in the

Caribbean Sea. It was late September. More than four months had passed since they had left Spain. Alonso de Ojeda was already there.

Two months later, Amerigo sailed to the Bahama Islands for the winter. In June, 1500, he finally returned to Spain. It had been a stormy voyage back across the Ocean Sea.

In thirteen months his ships had sailed 20,000 miles. He had mapped many new lands, stars and waters. He brought Queen Isabella gold, a huge sparkling emerald, a great purple amethyst and some pearls. She was delighted with her rare and beautiful gifts.

King Ferdinand was pleased with the maps Amerigo had made. So Amerigo gave one to the King in the shape of a globe. He also gave a copy of the globe and another map to Lorenzo di Pier in Florence.

"You are the best mapmaker in the world today," the King praised Amerigo.

Amerigo now was ill with jungle fever. He wanted to stay in Seville for a while with his wife and nephew. He hoped to return to the Indies when he was better, not for treasure, but to explore. He wanted to solve a mystery. Why was the Asia he had seen so different from the land described by Marco Polo?

8

Voyage for Portugal

A dusty Portuguese horseman galloped up to the Vespucci house in Seville. "King Emanuel of Portugal wishes to see Amerigo Vespucci at once!" he shouted.

Amerigo answered slowly, "A king's request is an order. I must go."

His nephew Giovanni cried eagerly, "I wish I could go to Portugal!"

Maria sighed. "Giovanni and I will live with my brother while you are gone,

Amerigo. Are you sure you feel well enough to make the trip?"

Amerigo rode away with the king's messenger. He wished he were feeling better. The jungle fever from the Indies still tired him. No one then knew the cause of malaria or how to cure it.

After days on horseback, Amerigo arrived at the Portuguese king's palace. "Our treaty with Spain gives Portugal all new land in the Indies east of a certain longitudinal line," King Emanuel told Amerigo. "You have already seen part of it. I am sending three ships to the Indies to claim and map this land. You will direct these ships and make the maps of the new Portuguese coast. You will have a good captain with you."

What Amerigo wanted most was to explore farther south than he had before.

Now he could solve the mystery of the Indies' golden cities. Now he might find a shorter route to the Indies than by sailing around Africa. During Amerigo's first voyage, Portugal's Vasco da Gama had returned home from India. He had reached India by sailing east around Africa. But it was a long, slow trip.

Amerigo's three ships sailed from Lisbon on May 13, 1501. Eleven days later, they docked at their first port, Dakar, Africa. Here they would get food, water and wood before their voyage west.

And here, to Amerigo's happy surprise, were two other Portuguese ships. "We come from the Indies," shouted the other seamen. "Our captain is Pedro Cabral."

Amerigo could hardly wait to question the seamen. Among them he found an old friend, the world traveler and geographer,

Gaspar. "We left Lisbon last year with sixteen ships," Gaspar said. "We were to sail east to the Indies around Africa."

Amerigo nodded. "Everyone in Portugal prayed for your safety."

"After leaving Dakar, we ran into bad weather," Gaspar went on. "We sailed west, to get out of the storm. We came to a strange land which seemed to be part of a continent. We claimed it for Portugal."

"It must be the coast I saw," Amerigo
answered. "Did it look like the Indies?"

Gaspar shook his head. "It didn't look
like India, or any Isles of the Indies that
we saw later." He sighed. "We lost five
ships and all on board, while we were
returning from the unknown coast to
Africa. But after reaching the Indies, we
found fabulous treasure. Come and see!"

Amerigo could hardly believe his eyes.
It was the richest cargo he had ever seen.

Besides perfumes, spices, drugs and beautiful woods, there were silks and satins, gold and diamonds, rubies and pearls.

"Did you see cities?" Amerigo asked.

"We saw crowded cities with shops and temples," Gaspar answered. "And we saw great animals in the jungle. There were tigers, lions and elephants."

Amerigo wrote at once to Lorenzo. "This voyage which I am now making is perilous to the limit of human courage," he wrote. But he was more excited than ever. He could tell no one of his latest idea, until he had proof. What if the new land to the west was not the Indies at all? Could it be an entirely new, unknown continent?

9

Commander of the Fleet

Rain drenched Amerigo's ships and sailors. Wind whistled through the sails. The three ships tossed and rolled, blown far off their course.

Portuguese sailors were better trained than Spanish sailors. Yet they understood little about navigation. Amerigo tried to teach them. Nevertheless, they were 64 days from Dakar before a sailor shouted, "Land ho!"

Amerigo looked carefully at the shore.

Yes, he had seen it before. It was the coast of Brazil. The explorers sailed on south, discovering new, beautiful land.

The jungle still extended to the ocean. Tall trees were gay with orchids. The air was full of perfume of flowers. Bright birds and butterflies flitted everywhere.

Sailing south, the Portuguese began to find breaks in the jungle. They left mirrors and bells on a sandy beach. Then they watched from their boats. Shy brown people stole from the forest to take the trinkets.

One day Amerigo landed with some men to explore inland. They made their way to a friendly village. For 27 days they lived with the Indians in a great thatched house. The whole village of 600 people lived there. The beds were nets of woven cotton swung from the ceiling.

"Such 'hammocks' would be good for sailors on board ship," Amerigo said.

The explorers liked the native food of wild cherries, shrimp, oysters, lobsters, roots, the meat of animals and birds. But they became sick when they saw human flesh drying in the sun. These people were cannibals.

Amerigo's men showed the natives bits of gold, silver and jewels. By signs they asked for more. The Indians shook their heads and pointed west. Then they pointed proudly to marble and crystal ornaments in their ears, lips and cheeks. These worthless stones and some gay feather crowns were their only treasures.

"Are these the richly dressed people of the Indies?" Amerigo answered his own question with a shake of the head.

Amerigo sailed on, naming new capes

and rivers. On January 1, 1502, the explorers saw the most beautiful harbor yet. Curving white sand beaches separated green mountains from blue sea. Amerigo named the bay "Rio de Janeiro," River of January.

The air grew cooler. The coast went southwest. From the stars, Amerigo could tell that he was in Spanish territory. The explorers landed for a meeting. "We are

now on Spanish, not Portuguese ground," the Captain said. "I cannot command the fleet here."

"Let Amerigo Vespucci command!" shouted a big sailor. "He is from Spain!"

"Amerigo Vespucci!" shouted all the seamen. And so Amerigo was chosen commander of the fleet in Spanish waters.

By now, Amerigo was almost sure that this continent was not Asia. It seemed to be a new continent between Africa and Asia. Perhaps he could sail around it into the Indian Ocean. Then there would be a new trade route to the Indies. "Sail on south!" he ordered.

The explorers landed at a wide river mouth. Again, by signs, they asked friendly natives for treasure. After seeing silver trinkets, the natives pointed up the river. And so Amerigo named the river

"Rio de la Plata," River of Silver. It is between today's Uruguay and Argentina.

Flat, rich land gave way to a rocky coast. There were few people. It was now April, which was spring in Europe. But it was fall here. A great storm raged for fifteen hours. Amerigo knew that worse winter weather lay ahead. He wrote in his notebook, "Finding ourselves in such peril, with such a storm that we could hardly see from one boat to another . . . we decided . . . to signal the fleet to assemble and set its course for Portugal." They were on the coast of today's Patagonia, almost at the southern tip of South America.

The leaking ships recrossed the Ocean Sea. On the African coast, the sailors repaired two ships. The third, which was beyond repair, was burned.

In September, 1502, Amerigo's two
ships arrived in Lisbon, Portugal. Only
one man had been lost. Amerigo had
been gone for sixteen months and had
explored 2,500 miles of new coast. He
could hardly wait to tell King Emanuel
about his discovery of more new land for
Portugal.

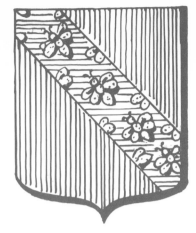

10

The New World

Amerigo Vespucci bowed before King Emanuel of Portugal. "Your Majesty," he said, "here are my notes and maps of the continent across the Ocean Sea."

The King took the papers. He glanced inside the notebook. "What is this?" he cried. "You think that . . .?"

Amerigo bowed again. "I think that the land I found is not Asia, but a new continent between Africa and Asia. Its people, products, plants and animals are different from those of Asia. Its longitude is not that of Asia. I have figured a new, scientific measurement of the earth. The world is much larger than scientists think. In two voyages, I have explored over 6,000 miles of the new coast."

King Emanuel stood in excitement. "And so you have found a New World!"

"I think I have," Amerigo answered.

The King threw his arms around Amerigo.

From Lisbon, Amerigo wrote to his old friend Lorenzo di Pier Francesco de Medici, in Florence, "We arrived at a new land which, for many reasons . . . we observed to be a continent." It was, he said, a New World.

In Florence, Lorenzo gave the letter to

Uncle Giorgio to read. Uncle Giorgio passed the letter to other leaders of the city. The rulers of Florence declared a carnival in Amerigo's honor.

For three nights the house where Amerigo was born was lighted from top to bottom. All Florence honored Amerigo with parades and parties. From that time, anyone in the Vespucci family could hang a special light at his door. Amerigo Vespucci had brought fame to his family.

Amerigo returned to his wife and Giovanni in Seville. "Oh, Amerigo," Maria cried, "you look so thin and yellow. Your fever is worse! Please do not make any more voyages."

Amerigo would not promise. He longed to explore again. Perhaps when he was feeling better, he could find the way past the New World to the Indies.

11

Pilot Major of Spain

A few years later, Amerigo Vespucci was invited once again to a king's court. This time, King Ferdinand of Spain wanted his help.

Before leaving Seville, Amerigo visited his good friend, Christopher Columbus. Columbus had just returned from his last voyage. The Admiral was old and ill. He gave Amerigo a letter for his son Diego, who was at court. Amerigo did not talk with Columbus about the New World. He knew that the Admiral still believed he had found the Indies.

King Ferdinand welcomed Amerigo as an honored guest. "Amerigo," the King said, "Spain is proud of your scientific work and exploration. We wish to make you a Capitano of Spain, to work for Seville's Board of Trade. You would oversee each Spanish expedition going to the New World. You would see to its food and other supplies. You would give it maps and plan its route. You would, of course, be well paid." He stopped, then asked, "Amerigo, if you accept this government job, would you also consider becoming a citizen of Spain?"

Amerigo thought quickly. He would like the work more than anything else, except to do the exploring himself.

Florence was no longer home to him, and no longer a center of science. His best friend in Florence, Lorenzo di Pier, had died. Amerigo's heart was now in Spain with his Spanish wife. His nephew wanted to stay in Seville. Spain had become the center of the exciting New World exploration.

Amerigo bowed. "I accept the work," .he said. "And I wish to become a Spanish citizen."

Amerigo soon received a royal letter of naturalization. He was a citizen and a Capitano of Spain.

Two busy years passed for Capitano Amerigo. Then King Ferdinand again called him to court. Spain's three best pilots were there too. They talked about trying to find the western route to Asia, past the southern tip of the New World.

Ships were being made ready for an expedition. Amerigo was planning their supplies. He was disappointed that other pilots would sail them.

Then Portugal learned about the new expedition. She said she would not allow ships to sail south along her Brazilian coast. "Surely the Portuguese will let *me* sail past the coast I discovered for them," Amerigo told the King. "May I go?"

"No," the King replied. "I cannot risk losing my best scientist."

The King had other work in mind for Amerigo. "Most Spanish pilots do not have enough training to take ships across the Ocean Sea," he said. "I want you to start a school for pilots. You will teach them to use the quadrant and the astrolabe. You will explain how to guide a ship by the stars. You will draw maps of the Ocean Sea and the New World for all pilots to use. They will report new discoveries to you for your map."

The King smiled at Amerigo, who stood silent with surprise. Then the King went on, "You will teach the pilots to figure latitude and longitude by the stars. No pilot may sail on a Spanish ship without a license from you." He smiled again. "Your title will be 'Pilot Major of Spain.' Your salary, of course, will be raised."

Amerigo bowed low. "Thank you, sire," he murmured. "It is a great honor."

The King's messengers galloped their horses to every town in Spain. They beat drums in each town square to call the people. Then they shouted, "All ship captains, mariners, pilots, and mates must attend the navigation school of Amerigo Vespucci in Seville!"

Amerigo opened the school in his home. Giovanni helped him with the map making and teaching. It was not easy to teach navigation to the seamen, for they had had little schooling. Amerigo could not teach them to tell longitude by the stars. Not even Giovanni could understand this. Only a few Portuguese scientists learned Amerigo's system.

Amerigo was now the best geographer of his time, one of the best scientists, and one of the most important men in Spain. He had another new title, "Astronomer to the King of Spain." Yet he still longed to explore. He wanted to find the waterway from the New World to Asia.

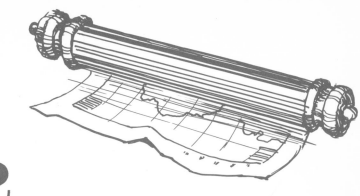

12

America Is Named

One day Giovanni burst into his Uncle Amerigo's classroom. "Great news!" he shouted.

Amerigo looked up in surprise, shaking his head at his nephew.

But nothing could stop Giovanni. He waved a map in the air. "I have a new map of the world!" the young man cried. "It is drawn by Martin Waldseemuller, map maker of Saint Dié Monastery in France! It shows the New World. And see!" Giovanni held up the map, pointing.

"He calls the New World's north coast, 'America,' in honor of you. (America was Amerigo's name in Latin.)

"He says here," Giovanni went on, " 'It is fitting that this fourth part of the world, inasmuch as Americus discovered it, should be called *Amerige* or *land of Americi* that is, *America.* ' "

Amerigo took the map, which had his picture on the border. All the seamen crowded around in great excitement. Amerigo smiled his old smile. "This is just one man's idea," he said. "Of course, it would be an honor if part of the coast I discovered had my name. But Columbus discovered the New World across the Ocean Sea, not I."

"You discovered that it is a new continent and not Asia. And you discovered most of its coast," Giovanni insisted as he rolled up the map. "You rightly deserve to have it called 'America' for you."

Soon copies of the monastery's new geography book and map were all over Europe. The monastery also printed Amerigo's letters to Florence about his explorations. They were translated from Italian into French, German and Latin. People everywhere read them and talked about them. What a wonderful place this New World must be! What wealth would come from it!

In Seville, Amerigo heard little more of the map's fame. He wished he had time to write a book about the New World. "It might make my name remembered," he thought. But Amerigo was too tired now to write the book from his notes.

The day came when Amerigo was too ill with malaria to teach. He died in 1512, when he was 58 years old. Just eight years later, Ferdinand Magellan, a Portuguese who sailed for Spain, discovered the passage to Asia. Amerigo had already pointed the way, around South America's Cape Horn.

Amerigo had discovered and mapped 6,000 miles of new coast, more than anyone else in the world's history. He had discovered new ocean currents, new stars and how to tell longitude at sea. He had discovered that Columbus' "Indies" were really a new continent between Europe and Asia.

Soon after Amerigo's death, the new southern continent he had explored was called "America." It was a good name, easy to say. And it went well with names of the other continents, Europe or Europa, Asia and Africa.

The southern continent had hardly been named before more explorers discovered more land, north of Columbus' Carribean islands. The new land was still another continent. It became "North America," and Amerigo's continent, "South America." And so, as his father had dreamed, Amerigo Vespucci's name became famous forever.

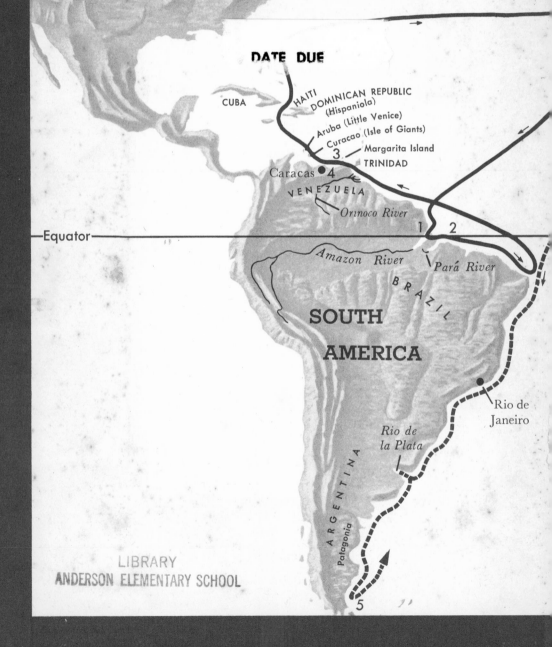

NORTH AMERICA

CUBA

HAITI

DOMINICAN REPUBLIC
(Hispaniola)

Aruba (Little Venice)

Curacao (Isle of Giants)

Margarita Island

3

TRINIDAD

Caracas ● 4

V E N E Z U E L A

Orinoco River

1   2

Equator

Amazon River

Pará River

B R A Z I L

SOUTH

AMERICA

Rio de
Janeiro

Rio de
la Plata

A
R
G
E
N
T
I
N
A

Patagonia

5